Savvy

Crafty Creations

Felting Projects
You Won't Be Able to
Resist

by Shalana Frisby

CAPSTONE PRESS
a capstone imprint

Savvy Books are published by Capstone Press,
1710 Roe Crest Drive, North Mankato, Minnesota 56003
www.mycapstone.com

Library of Congress Cataloging-in-Publication Data
Names: Frisby, Shalana, author.
Title: Felting projects you won't be able to resist / by Shalana Frisby.
Description: North Mankato, Minnesota: Capstone Press, 2018. | Series:
   Crafty creations | Audience: Ages 9–13.
Identifiers: LCCN 2017043046 (print) | LCCN 2017044402 (eBook) | ISBN
   9781515774525 (eBook PDF) | ISBN 9781515774488 (hardcover)
Subjects: LCSH: Felt work–Juvenile literature. | Felting–Juvenile
   literature.
Classification: LCC TT849.5 (eBook) | LCC TT849.5 .F75 2018 (print) | DDC
   746/.0463–dc23
LC record available at https://lccn.loc.gov/2017043046

Editorial Credits
Marissa Bolte, editor; Juliette Peters, designer; Sarah Schuette, photo stylist;
Marcy Morin, scheduler; Svetlana Zhurkin, media researcher; Kathy McColley,
production specialist

Photo Credits
All images by Capstone Studio/Karon Dubke except Shutterstock: Air Images, 22
(top), Dmitry Kalinovsky, cover (bottom), images72, 22 (bottom), tviolet, cover (top)

Printed and bound in the USA.
010845S18

Table of Contents

Get Felting!..4

    Starting Out: Felt Fabrics...................................6

    Synthetic Felt...7

Emotion Coasters 8

Pencil Case 10

Felt Box with Lid 12

Double-Sided Pinwheels for Hair Accessories.............14

Owl Pillow with Book Pocket 16

    The Wooly Truth 22

    Feel It: Wool Felt 24

    Wet Felting 26

    Needle Felting 28

Balls and Pennant Flags Banner.........................30

Cord Bracelets..34

Shadow Box Art 38

Tic, Tac, and Go! 42

    Read More..48

    Author Bio 48

    Titles in This Set 48

Get Felting!

Felt is fun! Felt comes in both brightly colored sheets and natural wool fibers. You can make almost anything out of felt – and have lots of fun doing it!

Did you know that there are not only several kinds of felt, but that they all have very different characteristics? Some are synthetic fabrics, like the kind that make up the sheets you see in the craft stores. Some types of traditional felt you actually have to make yourself from natural wool. That comes almost straight from a sheep! All felt materials are known for their soft, plush texture. Each kind of felt has its own purpose in the world of crafting.

You can make your own felted crafts through wet felting and needle felting. The techniques are different in both their tools and methods. But both create interesting crafts of all kinds, from flat surface pictures to sculpted animals.

5

Starting Out: Felt Fabrics

Felt fabrics are premade sheets of matted material. There are synthetic felt fabrics, all-natural wool felt fabrics, and combination blends made of both types. Felt fabrics can be treated like any other material and can be cut, sewn, and even glued.

Synthetic Felt

Most people are very familiar with synthetic felt fabrics. They are made by a machine, and from man-made fibers such as polyester, acrylic, or rayon. Common in craft stores, they are usually seen as 9-by-12 inch (23-by-30.5 centimeter) craft felt sheets. They are also sold on bolts, like fabric. This is called by-the-yard felt. Synthetic felt fabrics are budget-friendly to purchase and come in a wide variety of colors and patterns.

Stiffened felt is firmer and works well for 3D projects. You can buy stiffened craft felt, or you can make your own — just mix a combination of one part white glue and one part warm water. Soak the felt well, and then gently squeeze to remove any excess liquid. Set the felt pieces on baking sheets or on a wax paper-lined work surface, and let it dry completely. Remove wrinkles by ironing between two towels.

Essential Tools:

white glue

warm water

bowl

baking sheet or wax paper-lined surface

iron

towels

Emotion Coasters

Let everyone know how you are feeling with these fun coasters. Use by-the-yard felt to invent and discover new faces and emotions!

Materials

no-sew iron-on permanent adhesive felt sheet

6-inch (15.2-cm) square black felt

4-inch (10.2-cm) square red felt

two-sided fusible interfacing, medium weight

two 9-inch (23-cm) square or larger pieces yellow felt

iron and cotton cloth or towel

1 Cut pieces of the adhesive sheet to match the black and red felt pieces. Follow the package directions to attach the adhesive. Leave the paper backing on the sheets.

2 Cut a piece of fusible interfacing to match the yellow felt. Follow the package directions and sandwich the interfacing between the two pieces of felt.

3 Trace and cut out four 4-inch circles onto the yellow felt.

4 Cut two hearts out of the red felt.

5 Draw and cut out eye and mouth shapes on the black felt.

6 Arrange eye and mouth pieces on the yellow circles. When you're happy with how they look, remove the paper backings on the small pieces. Use the iron to glue them in place.

Tip:

When ironing synthetic felt fabric or sheets, always use a thin cotton cloth or towel between the felt and iron. The cloth will help keep the felt from melting. Keep moving the iron as you use it, and don't set your iron above medium-high.

9

Pencil Case

A simple stitch is usually enough to keep your projects together. The running stitch and whip stitch are easy stitches that everyone should learn.

Running Stitch:

Running stitches are great basic stitches. Poke the needle through the underside of the fabric. Pull the thread through the fabric, and then poke the needle back through. This is a stitch. Continue making small stitches in a straight line.

Whip Stitch:

Whip stitches are useful for joining fabric edges. Poke the needle through the underside of the fabric. Pull it all the way through. Poke the needle through the underside again, next to your first stitch. Continue looping the stitches until your pieces are joined.

This handy pencil case can be hooked to a keychain or inside a bag or backpack. It is just the right size to hold your essentials on the way to class.

Materials

sheet of felt

iron

¾-inch- (19-millimeter-) wide hook and loop fastener

7/8-inch- (22-mm-) wide grosgrain ribbon

needle and thread or sewing machine

Note:

There are some drawbacks to using synthetic felt. Craft felt sheets are thin and not made for long-lasting projects.

Using by-the-yard felt instead will make this project a little more durable, but either can be used.

1 Cut the felt into a 9-by-4-inch (23-by-10.2-cm) piece. Fold it in half the long way, and use an iron to make the fold crisp.

2 Cut a 1-inch- (2.5 cm-) long slit down the creased fold on one end. This is the top of the pencil case.

3 Unfold the felt. Cut a 1 ¾-inch (4.4-cm) piece of hook and loop fastener. Line it up with the top edge of the felt, and stitch into place.

4 Cut a piece of ribbon 7 inches (17.8-cm) long. Turn each end in about 1/2 inch (1.3 cm), and iron flat. Then stitch along the creases.

5 Fold the ribbon in half lengthwise. Use the iron to make the fold crisp.

6 Line the edges of the ribbon along the top of the felt. The folded end of the ribbon should stick out a little. Stitch the ribbon to the felt. You can use the loop to hang your pencil case off a key ring or binder.

7 Fold the felt in half again. Stitch around the bottom and side, about ¼ inch (0.6 cm) from the edge. Stop when you get to the looped ribbon handle.

Felt Box with Lid

When making this unique treasure box, get creative! Attach beads, buttons, paper flowers, and more to decorate each box. Make the pattern larger for a bigger box.

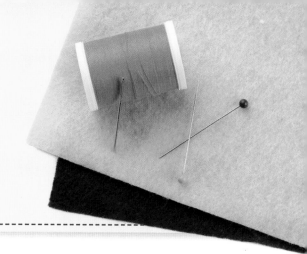

Materials

paper and pencil

ruler

9-by-12-inch (23-by-30.5-cm) stiffened craft felt sheet

sewing pins

needle and thread

For the Box:

1 Draw a square on the piece of paper. The square should have 2 ½-inch (6.4-cm) sides.

2 Add four more squares of the same size. Each square should share one side with the original square, to make a plus-sign shape. Cut out the pattern.

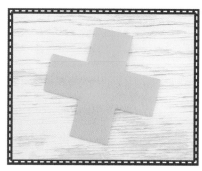

For the Lid:

1 Draw a square with 2 3/4-inch (7-cm) sides.

2 Add four rectangles. Each rectangle should share one side with the original square. The rectangles should measure 2 ¾-by-¾-inches (7-by-2-cm). Cut out the pattern.

To Assemble:

1 Trace the patterns for the box and the lid onto stiffened craft felt.

2 Cut out the shapes, and crease the folds along the center squares' edges.

3 Pin two edges of the box together, and use a needle and thread to stitch along the edges.

4 Continue pinning and stitching until all four seams are sewn.

5 Repeat steps 3 and 4 for the lid.

Double-Sided Pinwheels for Hair Accessories

Tip:

Using a rotary cutter, cutting mat, and quilting ruler will make this project go much more quickly. All are available at craft stores.

With these pinwheels, you'll bring a bit of the outdoors with you wherever you go! Make multiple pinwheels and use them to dress up pillows and birthday banners. They can even be made in the colors of your favorite school or sports team to wear to the next big game.

Materials (for one)

iron

4-inch (10.2-cm) square of by-the-yard felt in your choice of color

4-inch square of cotton fabric in your choice of pattern

two-sided fusible interfacing, medium weight

chalk and ruler

needle and embroidery thread

button

hair band

1 Iron the felt and the fabric squares.

2 Cut one piece of fusible interfacing to match the squares. Follow the package instructions to sandwich the interfacing between the felt and fabric.

3 Trim all the sides of the square to reduce it to 3 inches (7.6 cm).

4 Use the chalk and ruler to draw two diagonal lines on the felt. The center of the pinwheel is where the lines meet. Make a mark about 1/3 of the way up from the center of each line..

5 Starting at the corners, cut along the diagonal lines. Stop at the chalk marks you made.

6 Fold each corner point in toward the center. Stitch each corner into place.

7 Center a hair band underneath the pinwheel. Stitch a button to the top of the pinwheel, and loop the thread around the hair band several times to keep it in place.

Owl Pillow with Book Pocket

Tuck your favorite book into this cozy felt pillow. First, cut out the body. Then decorate the pocket. Add eyes and a beak, and you're done! You can switch out the colors to customize it. Add an array of rainbow colored felt feathers — and a book! — if you like.

Materials

- 1/2 yard (0.46 meters) of brown felt
- 1/3 yard (0.3 m) of light brown felt
- sewing pins
- iron
- needle and thread or sewing machine
- chalk
- 1/8 yard (0.1 m) each of teal felt and gold felt
- sewable iron-on adhesive sheet
- small pieces of off-white felt and orange felt
- compass
- two 1-inch (2.5-cm) or larger black buttons
- needle and embroidery thread
- pillow stuffing

For the Pocket:

1 Cut an 11-by-9 ½-inch (28-by-24-cm) piece out of the light brown felt. This will be the pocket.

2 Fold one of the long sides of the pocket piece over ½ inch (1.3 cm). Pin the fold in place, or use an iron to make a crease. Stitch about 1/8 inch (0.3 cm) from the cut edge. This will make the top of the pillow pocket.

3 Measure and mark 4 inches (10.2 cm) down from the top left corner of the pocket. Then mark 2 inches (5 cm) in from there. Repeat on the right side.

4 Repeat step 3, but start 3 inches (7.6 cm) from the top corners. Repeat again at 2 inches and 1 inch (2.5 cm).

5 Use chalk to draw a straight 7-inch (17.8-cm) line between the 4-inch marks. Repeat between the 3-inch marks and the 2-inch marks.

Continued on the next page...

6 Next, cut the feathers from the teal and gold felt. Cut 15 triangles – nine of one color, six of the other. They should be 3 inches wide and 3 inches tall.

7 Lay one row of feathers, three triangles across, on the pocket. Use the color you have more of. The short edge of the triangles should line up with the lowest long chalk mark you made in step 3. Pin and sew the feathers into place.

8 Lay another row of feathers over the first, using the other color this time. They should line up with the 3-inch line.

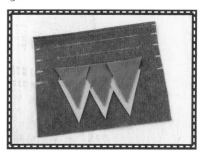

9 Repeat step 8 at the 2-inch line, the 1-inch line, and at the top of the pocket. Alternate rows of feather colors.

For the Owl:

1 Cut two 11-by-16-inch (18-by-40.6-cm) pieces of brown felt.

2 Set one piece of felt face-up on your work surface. Place the pocket piece over the top of the body. The bottom edges and sides should line up.

Continued on the next page...

Continued on the next page...

19

3 Pin the pocket in place, and sew the three edges to the body. Leave a ½-inch seam allowance on all the sides.

4 To make the eyes, apply iron-on adhesive to the back of the off-white felt. Use a compass to trace and cut out two 3-inch-wide circles.

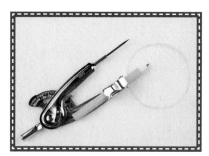

5 Center the eyes about 2 ½ inches (6.6 cm) from the top of one of the pieces of brown felt. Use an iron to stick on the eyes.

6 Apply iron-on adhesive to the back of the orange felt. Cut a small triangle to make a beak.

7 Center the beak slightly over the eyes, and attach with the iron.

8 Place the buttons on top of the off-white felt, to make eyes. Sew them into place.

To Turn it Into a Pillow:

1 Set the back piece of the owl's body over the front piece, wrong-side-up. Pin the edges together, and then sew most of the way around. Leave the last few inches unsewn.

2 Turn the owl right-side-out. Straighten all the sides, and then stuff until the pillow is full.

3 Fold in the open edge of the pillow and sew it shut.

Tip:

Take a shortcut and skip the owl instructions. Just make a simple pillow with a pocket instead. Have fun choosing colors!

The Wooly Truth

Now that you've had the chance to experiment with synthetic felt, it's time to dig into the real thing!

Wool roving is the key fabric in both wet felting and needle felting. Roving resembles a long, thick piece of brushed hair – and that's exactly what it is. When wool is taken from sheep or other wool-producing animals, it is cut from the animals (without harming them), and cleaned of oil and dirt. Then it is combed in a method called carding. A carding machine with fine needlelike teeth acts like a hairbrush to align all the fibers in one direction and smooth the wool into long pieces of roving.

When roving is separated and stacked in layers, it can be agitated through either wet or needle felting methods to lock the fibers together. From there it becomes flat sheets or dimensional shapes, such as balls or squares. It can also be prepared in different ways for spinning. All of these types of roving work well for both needle and wet felting, and they can be found in both smaller quantities at craft stores and larger quantities online.

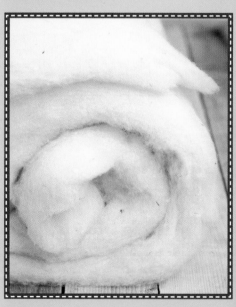

How to Handle Wool Roving

To pull wool from a long strand of roving, wrap one hand about 6 inches (15 cm) from the end and hold tightly. Then carefully pull from the end with your other hand to loosen the fibers. You should pull out a thin layer of wispy fibers. This is the correct way to remove wool from a piece of roving.

Thicker pieces of wool roving may need to be separated or split in half for easier pulling.

Tip:

Never, ever cut roving before it's felted! This will damage the fibers by shortening them and causing blunt ends. Always pull fibers from a strand of roving.

Feel It: Wool Felt

Wool felt is made of 100 percent natural fibers from sheep, alpaca, or other wool-producing animals. This type of fabric has been cleaned, processed, and machine-woven into sheets of matted material. Wool felt fabrics can be purchased by the sheet and by the yard.

Wool felt fabrics are thicker and more durable than synthetic felt fabrics. They are also heat resistant and breathe well, making them much better for clothing and wearable projects. But they are less commonly used in projects because of their availability and expense.

Most craft stores do not carry all-wool fabric. And it can also be much more expensive than synthetic felt material to purchase. Don't let this hold you back from using it for the right project, though! Look online or at your local fabric or yarn store.

Wet Felting

In the wet felting process, segments of wool roving are stacked in thin crisscrossing layers to help the fibers cling to one another. Then heat – usually in the form of hot, soapy water – is applied to the layered wool. Finally, gentle agitation is applied to help mat the wool fibers together.

During the hand felting process, the surface area will shrink by one-quarter to one-third of its original size. The result is dense felt fabric, balls, or cords. This simple and ancient technique has made everything from tents to clothes to shoes for people throughout the ages.

When preparing to **wet felt**, gather all the essential tools on a waterproof surface, such as a plastic bin or large sink basin. In your bowl, mix very warm water – as hot as you can stand – with a few drops of dish soap. Place wool roving in a dry area away from water until you're ready to use it.

Essential Tools:

wool roving

mild dish soap

bowl of hot water

waterproof work surface, such as a shallow plastic bin

bubble wrap

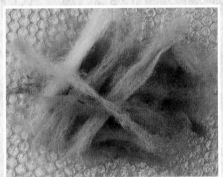

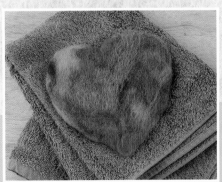

Tip:

When wet felting, the hotter the water, the better – but make sure it's not too hot for your hands. A drop or two of dish soap is all you need. A few suds are OK, but you should be able to see the wool through the suds as you work.

Tip:

Bubble wrap makes wet felting easier. Its waterproof surface and textured base help speed up the felting process. It also makes the process easier on your hands. You can use other durable waterproof materials, such as plastic bags, pieces of tarp, or bamboo mats. There are also plastic mats made specifically for felting work. But bubble wrap is the cheapest and easiest material to find.

Needle Felting

The needle felting technique, sometimes called dry felting, uses specially made felting needles. The needles have a long, barbed edge to intertwine wool fibers. Their tiny barbs lift the wool up and down as you stab at it, interlocking the fibers. A foam pad or thick soft material is placed underneath for a work surface.

While shrinkage still occurs as the fibers mat together, it is usually less than when wet felting. Needle felting is amazingly versatile and can produce flat objects, surface design, and adorable 3D animals. Supplies are available at most major craft stores and online.

For **needle felting**, gather all the essential tools on a hard, flat surface. Be sure to keep your felting needles in a safe, visible spot nearby.

Essential Tools:

wool roving

felting needles (fine and medium gauge)

piece of foam at least 2 inches (5 cm) tall, such as a square pillow foam insert

bubble wrap

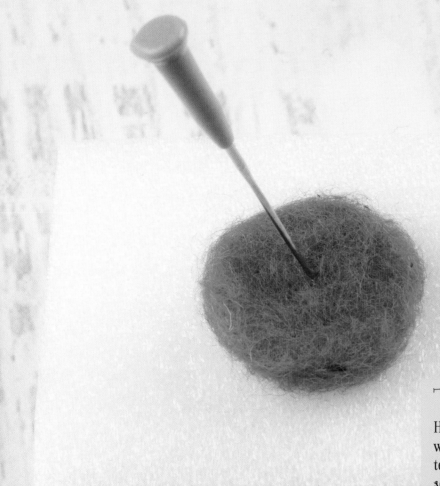

Tip:

Have an adult help you with needle felting techniques. And do it somewhere quiet – you don't want to get distracted and accidentally stab yourself! When using the needle, poke it straight up and down.

29

Balls and Pennant Flags Banner

Add some adorable flair to your room decor or a class party with this miniature banner of felted wool balls and easy-to-cut flags. Customize it by adding stick-on felt letters to the flags with your name. You can also substitute colorful pom-poms for the wet felted balls to make it an even quicker craft project.

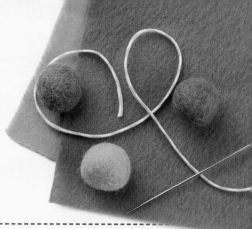

Materials

two or more coordinating colors of wool roving, about 2 feet (0.6 m) of each

mild dish soap and hot water

two 3-by-6-inch (7.6-by-15.2-cm) pieces of by-the-yard felt in different colors

1 1/2 yards (1.4 m) of colored cord

yarn needle and thimble

For the Wool Balls:

1 Separate a strand of wool roving about ½ inch (1.3-cm) wide and 2 feet long. Set it on a dry surface.

2 Fold over one end of the strand a few times, and pinch it into a wad. Wrap tight, criss-crossing layers of roving around the wad to form a ball.

3 Once the ball is tightly wrapped, hold it together and dip it in the hot, soapy water. When it is completely soaked, remove it and firmly roll it between the palms of your hands.

4 Continue to dip and roll. At first, the ball will feel loose, but eventually the fibers will begin to mat together. You'll know it's felted when the surface is smooth and spongy, with a hard middle.

5 When the ball is felted, rinse it well in cold water and set aside to dry.

6 Repeat steps 1–5 to make six more balls.

Continued on the next page...

For the Flags:

1 Cut three flags from each of the felt sheets. The flags should measure 3 inches wide and 3 inches tall.

To Assemble the Banner:

1 Tie a double knot about 8 inches (20.3 cm) from one end of the cord. Thread the other end with the yarn needle.

2 Push the needle through a wool ball to thread it onto the cord. Use the thimble to protect your fingertip.

3 Thread a flag onto the cord. Leave about an inch between each ball and flag.

4 Continue threading wool balls and flags until you reach the end of the cord. After the last ball, double knot the end of the cord, and cut an 8-inch tail.

Tip:

An alternative to wet felting the wool balls is needle felting. Do steps 1 and 2, but then skip wet felting. Instead, use a felting needle to poke the fibers into shape. Continue poking – carefully! – until a smooth ball is formed. For the smoothest surface, use a medium-gauge felting needle first and then a fine-gauge needle to finish.

Cord Bracelets

Make bangle bracelets for yourself and all your friends. Better yet, throw a fun bracelet-making party for this quick and easy wet felting craft!

Materials

wool roving, about 2 feet (0.6 m) long

hot, soapy water

two sheets of bubble wrap

needle and embroidery thread

buttons, beads, or other embellishments

1 Separate a piece of roving about 1-inch- (2.5-cm-) wide.

2 Fold the strip in half lengthwise, and rub it gently between the palms of your hands to form a snake.

3 Wet the cord in hot, soapy water until it's completely soaked. Place the cord between the sheets of bubble wrap, and press firmly on it before you start felting.

4 When the fibers start to mat together, remove the cord from the bubble wrap. Use the palms of your hands to rub the cord back and forth from one end to the other. Press firmly as you go, and re-dip in the water if needed.

5 The cord will shrink and become more dense as you roll. It should be fully felted in about 15 minutes.

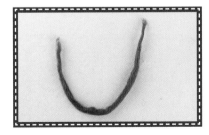

6 Rinse the cord in cold water to remove all the soap, and set aside to dry.

Continued on the next page...

35

7 To make a bracelet, wrap the dry cord around your wrist. Then add an inch. Cut the ends of the cord as needed.

8 Use a needle and embroidery thread to sew the ends of the cord together. Sew on buttons or beads to decorate.

Tip:

Combine multiple colors of roving strands side-by-side to make striped bracelet cords. You can also add dots or other patterns to the bracelets by needle felting bits of wool roving directly onto the cords.

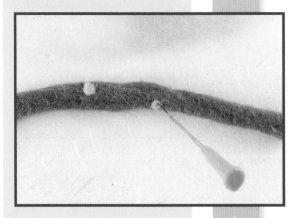

TRY THIS

Add some stability: Felt the wool around a heavier gauge craft wire.

Thread beads onto the bracelets before closing the bracelet wire with loops. Use jump rings to attach charms, or head pins to add beads.

Use end caps to close your bracelets instead of beads.

TRY THIS

Layer several different colors for a floral look. Then slice through the roving to make beads. Use a needle to string them onto beading cord.

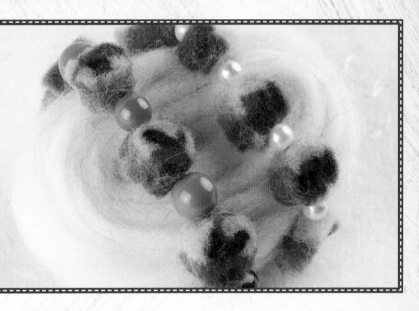

TRY THIS

Use a needle and thread to sew seed beads onto the bracelet.

Shadow Box Art

Take scrapbooking to the next level and leave a message (or a memory) in a shadow box instead!

Materials

2-inch (5-cm) round cookie cutter

needle felting foam

8-inch (20.3-cm) piece of white wool roving

medium-gauge felting needle

fine-gauge felting needle

1 ½-inch (3.8-cm) round cookie cutter

8-inch piece of red wool roving

24-gauge (or smaller) black wire

12-inch (30.5-cm) piece of ribbon, ¼-inch- (6.4-mm-) wide

small paper tag

letter stickers

clear industrial-strength glue

double-sided tape

large glue dots

8-inch square piece of light blue cardstock

8-inch square shadow box frame

To Make the Clouds:

1 Lay the 2-inch cookie cutter on the foam pad. Fill the cookie cutter with a few criss-crossing layers of white roving. Tuck any wispy fibers inside the cookie cutter's edge.

2 Use a medium-gauge felting needle to poke the layered wool repeatedly. It will resemble a big, fluffy hairball at first – don't be discouraged, though. Just keep going!

3 After a few minutes, the wool will start to mat together and feel spongy to the touch. Flip the circle over inside the cookie cutter and continue poking the other side.

4 When the circle has the feel of a dense fabric and most wispy fibers are matted down, remove the cookie cutter. Carefully rotate the circle between your fingers. Use the fine-gauge needle to poke any stray fibers and sculpt the edges.

5 Repeat steps 1-4 to make five more white circles.

6 Overlap the circles however you like to make a fun cloud shape. Use the medium-gauge felting needle to poke the wool and mat the circles together. Continue sculpting the cloud with a fine-gauge needle until you are happy with how it looks.

Continued on the next page...

39

To Make the Balloons:

1 Using the 1 ½-inch cookie cutter and red wool, follow the directions for making the clouds to make three red circles.

2 Use the medium-gauge needle to sculpt a circle into a balloon shape. Pinch the edge of each circle to form a teardrop shape.

3 Poke repeatedly at the pinched edge of the teardrop to make a balloon lip. Use your fingers to flare the balloon lip and flatten its round top.

4 Switch to the fine-gauge needle to finish shaping the balloon's surface. Repeat this process to shape all the red circles into balloons.

To Assemble the Shadow Box:

1 Cut an 8-inch piece of black wire for each balloon. Wrap one end of wire around each balloon, just above the lip. Twist to secure it. Gather the other ends of the wire strands together to make a balloon bouquet. Vary the length of the strands.

2 Gather the wires together at the center. Tie the ribbon into a bow, wrapping it around the gathered spot.

3 Decorate the paper tag with letter stickers, or just write your own note. Thread the tag onto one of the ribbon tails. Trim the other tail shorter.

Finish

Use a combination of clear industrial-strength glue, double-sided tape, and glue dots to attach the clouds, balloons, ribbon, and tag to the light blue cardstock. Insert the cardstock into the shadowbox frame.

Materials Note:

Felting needles come in a variety of sizes and shapes. For this project, you will need a medium-gauge needle (size 36) to start and a fine-gauge needle (size 38) to finish. Always begin with coarser gauge needles and finish with finer gauge needle to tuck in the last of the wispy fibers and finish off with a smooth look. A multineedle holding tool is not necessary, but it does help speed up the process.

Tic, Tac, and Go!

In the car, at the park, even at a restaurant, this little tic-tac-toe game will come in handy when you are on the go. Not only is it an adventure in wet felting to make, it also easily rolls up to go with you almost anywhere. And you can tell everyone that you made it from sheep's wool!

Materials

two 12-inch (30.5 cm) pieces of bubble wrap

plastic bin

white or light-colored wool roving, about 4 feet (1.2 m) long

brightly colored wool roving, about 2 ½ feet (0.8 m) long

hot, soapy water

two 10-inch- (25.4-cm) long pieces of 1/8-inch- (3.2-mm-) wide ribbon

matching embroidery thread with needle

colored paint pens

ten 1 ¼-inch (3.2-cm) wooden discs

1 Set one sheet of bubble wrap, bubble side-up, in the plastic bin. Lay two criss-crossing layers of colored wool roving on top. Leave about ½ inch (1.3 cm) of space around the edge.

2 Add three more criss-crossing layers of white roving over the colored layers. Tuck in any wispy edges. It will look like a high, fluffy blanket of loose fibers at this point.

3 Separate out four more ½-by-12-inch (1.3-by-30.5-cm)-thick sections of colored wool roving. Gently rub each between your palms to tuck in any wispy fibers.

4 Set the colored wool segments onto the layered wool in the bin to make a tic-tac-toe board. With dry hands, press the fluffy layers of wool together gently with your flat palms.

5 Soak the flat sheet of wool by gently sprinkling it with hot, soapy water. Continue until it is evenly wet all over. Make sure the fibers don't separate. If they do, gently position them back in place.

Continued on the next page...

43

There are many variations of this method to wet felt wool. These instructions show one tried and true way to make a felted wool sheet. In order to wet felt, you need three things: layered wool fibers, heat (warm, soapy water), and agitation (applying pressure). The bubble wrap keeps the fibers aligned and intact while they are felting, and the soap helps lubricate the fibers for movement.

Some people substitute bamboo mats for bubble wrap and use dry flake soap instead of plain dish soap. Many different methods can lead to the same result. Do a bit of research and enjoy figuring out what works best for you!

6 When the wool is completely wet and dripping, the fibers should naturally begin to flatten against each other. Use the palms of your hands to gently press the fibers down further. Then place the other piece of bubble wrap over the top of the wet wool sheet.

7 Continue pressing on the bubble wrapped-wool. Tuck in any bulging edges as you go, and be careful not to pop the bubble wrap. Press for about 5 minutes, or until the fibers begin to cling to each other.

8 Carefully flip over your bubble wrap and wool sandwich. Then press the top side for 5 minutes. Lift the top layer of bubble wrap occasionally to check the fibers and to wet the wool as needed. If the wool is too wet, drain any excess water.

9 Flip the sandwich over every 5 minutes, and keep felting. After about 30 minutes, the wool sheet will be matted but still very spongy to the touch.

10 When the sheet is matted well and no thin fibers pull up from the surface or shift when touched, you can remove it from the bubble wrap.

11 Keep felting! Work the sheet with your hands for another 15 to 20 minutes. Pretend it's dough! You should also throw it against a hard surface – like a sink basin – a few times to shock the wool. Then keep kneading! The wool should become denser and lose its spongy quality. You will also notice it shrinking in size.

Continued on the next page...

12 When the surface of the sheet starts to wrinkle a bit and it has the dense feel of a thick blanket, it is fully felted. Rinse it with cold water for a few minutes. Press (don't wring) out any excess water, and lay it on a towel to air dry. Use your hands to pull and smooth out any surface wrinkles.

13 Fold the pieces of ribbon in half, and pin them to the top of the game board. Then stitch them in place. When you're not using your board, you can roll it up and use the ribbon to keep it shut.

To Create the Game Pieces:

1 While the felt board is drying, make game pieces to go along with it! Use a paint pen to draw X's and O's on the wooden discs. Let them dry completely before playing.

You can use anything you want for your X's and O's! Try two colors of felted wool balls, or paint rocks to match your wool. What about making mini Emotion Coasters?

Read More

Blum, Nicole, and Catherine Newman. *Stitch Camp.* North Adams, Mass.: Storey Publishing, 2017.

Kuskowski, Alex. *Cool Needle Felting for Kids: A Fun and Creative Introduction to Fiber Art.* Minneapolis: ABDO Publishing Company, 2015.

Author Bio

Shalana Frisby has been a fiber artist and feltmaker for more than 10 years. She began her writing career as a blogger at her site, TheFunkyFelter.com, and has sold her fiber arts and other handmade goods at craft shows across the nation. She is also the former craft editor for *Country Woman* magazine, *Birds and Blooms* magazine, and *Taste of Home* magazine and books. Her craft instructions and creations have been featured in dozens of national print publications as well as online and on television. Shalana is currently a freelance writer and editor and enjoys time with her husband and daughter at home in the beautiful Ozarks region of southern Missouri.

Titles in This Set

Crochet Projects That Will Hook You

Felting Projects You Won't Be Able to Resist

Knitting Projects You'll Purl Over

Seamless Sewing Projects